What could be more  on a puppet show? First, think of a story you know or make up your own. After that, make puppets. Finally, ask friends, mothers, fathers, sisters, and brothers to come see your play.

In this book, you'll learn how to make two different kinds of puppets for "Little Red Riding Hood." Change the colors and other parts to fit the story *you* want to tell.

The Wolf: An Origami Puppet

paper	markers
scissors	glue

1. Fold the paper's top left corner over so its top edge is even with the right side of the page.

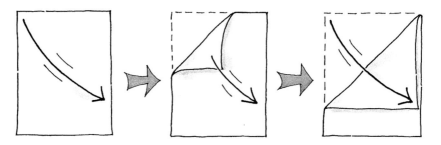

2. Cut off the part under the triangle. Save that scrap.

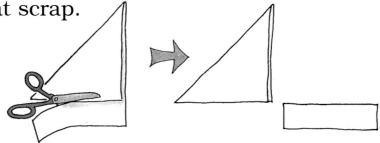

3. Open the triangle. Color the square you formed gray. Refold the page into a triangle again with the gray on the outside.

4. Bring the bottom left corner up to touch the top corner.

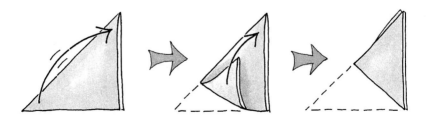

5. Turn the triangle so that only one point is at the bottom. Fold down the top right corner. Then fold the tip back up. Do the same for the other side.

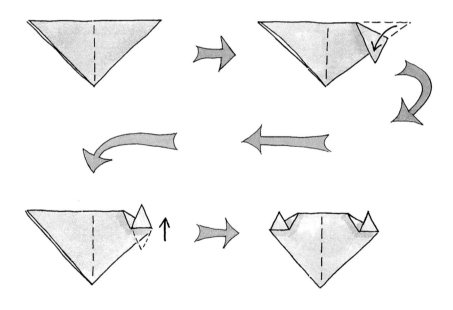

6. Take the scrap paper. Draw two
triangles for the ears and color them
pink. Draw two eyes, fangs, and a black
nose. Cut out these parts and glue
them to your puppet.

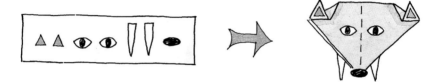

7. Pull up the front fold. Crease it so that
it stands up. Move the puppet by
pulling and pushing near its ears.

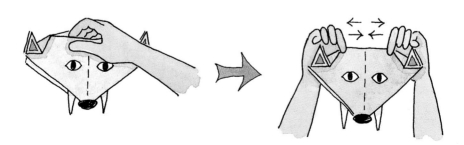

Red Riding Hood: A String Puppet

2 paper tubes (small, big)
paper punch, fasteners
paper, posterboard, felt
markers, glue, string

1. Cover the small tube with paper that goes with what your character wears.

2. Draw and cut out all other needed parts, such as the cape, arms, legs, and a head with a long neck.

3. Punch holes as shown.

4. Push paper fasteners through the holes. Go from outside each part to inside the tube. Start with the arms, legs, and head.

7

5. Measure three lengths of string, about 12 inches each. Tie a string around each end of the big tube. Tie one around the middle too.

Now tie the end strings to the puppet's arms. Tie the middle string to its head. Add any other parts of this character's costume.